To NICOLE,

Enjoy!

[signature]

hi·stories®

THOMOOSE
JEFFERSON

Based on the life of the great inventor and statesman, Thomas Jefferson

Written and Illustrated by:
ANDREW TOFFOLI

THOMOOSE JEFFERSON

Copyright © **The Little Germ That Could... Creations**, 2012

All Rights Reserved

Printed in China

ISBN 978-0-9763233-9-6

Library of Congress Control Number: 2012900892

**Our mission is to educate children about history
while using humor and imagination to teach valuable life lessons.**

Please visit us online at: **www.littlegerm.com**

10 9 8 7 6 5 4 3 2 1

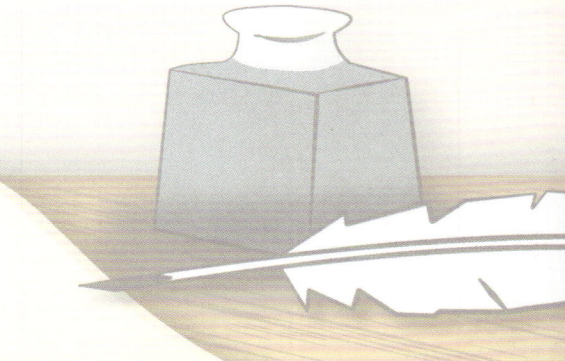

For Bingo

Thomoose Jefferson,
a studious moose,
was born at
Shadwell Plantation, Virginia,
in 1743.

Thomoose loved going to school,

3

and collecting books.

Thomoose exclaimed, "Reading helped me become a self-taught polyglot! I learned how to speak French, Spanish, Italian, Latin and Greek."

Thomoose went to college and studied very hard to become a lawyer.

7

After law school, he began to look for a home,
but could not find a place to call his own.

He finally found a piece of land
and designed a house that would be quite grand.

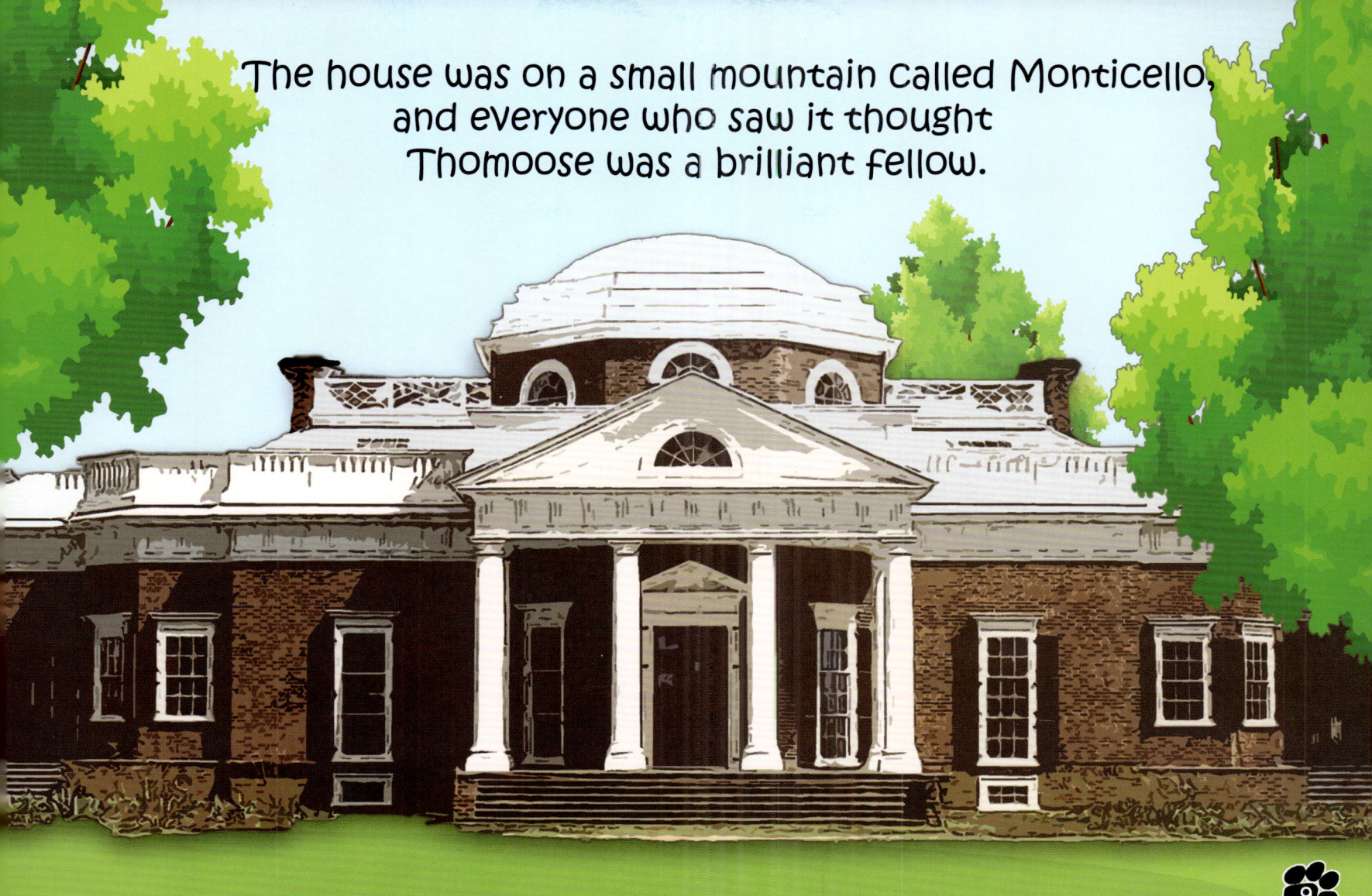

The house was on a small mountain called Monticello,
and everyone who saw it thought
Thomoose was a brilliant fellow.

Early in his career, Thomoose went to Philadelphia to help the Continental Congress defend the colonies against Britain's "Intolerable Acts."

Thomoose then added,
"The colonies are
prepared to fight
to defend what is right!"

12

The colonists continued to disagree with Britain until they could take no more and started the Revolutionary War.

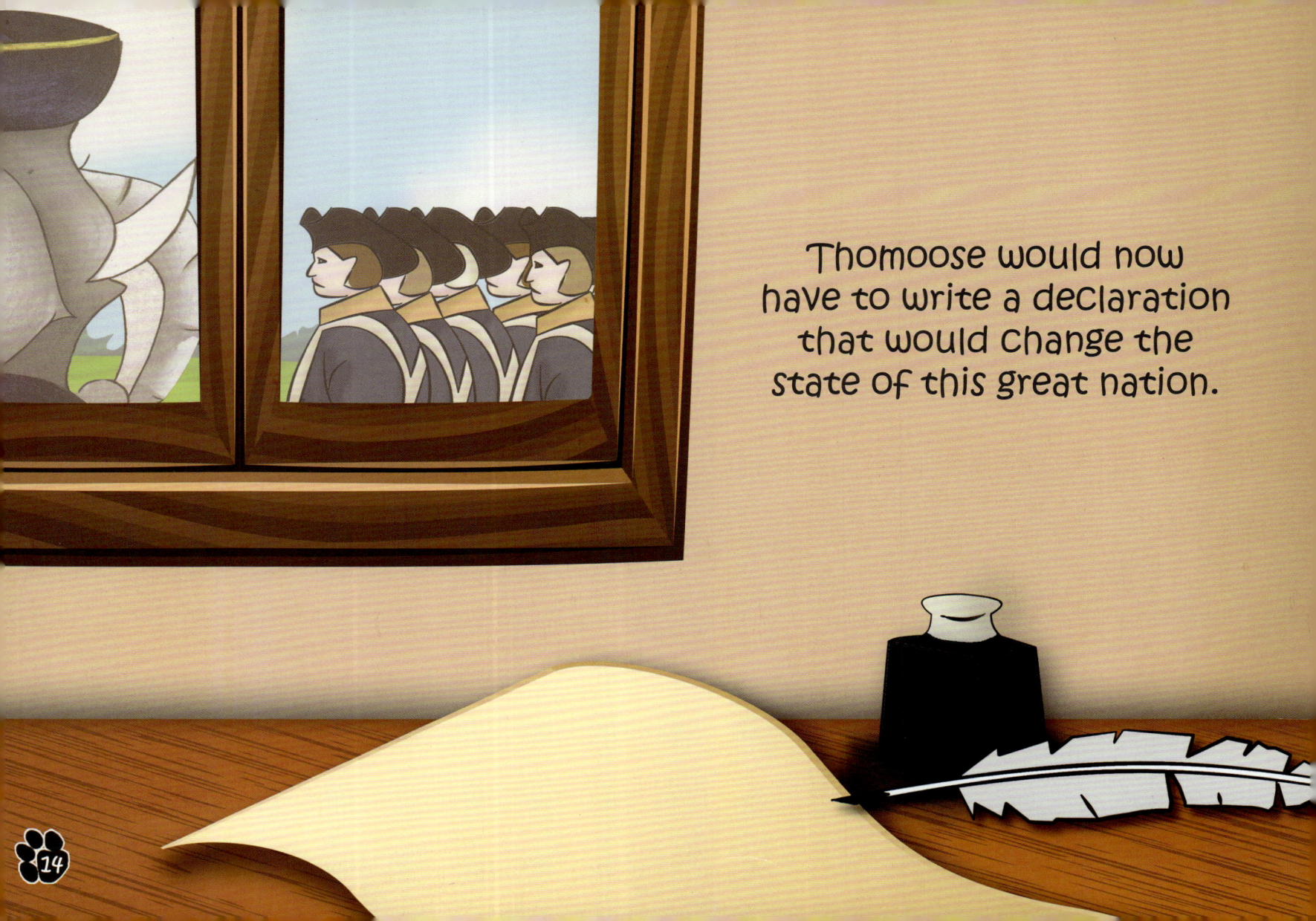

Thomoose would now have to write a declaration that would change the state of this great nation.

The Declaration of Independence stated that the Colonies would now be free independent states.

15

It stated that all men
were created equal...

...and they wanted to
let the king
know that they were
no longer under his control.

It stated that every person in the United States had a right to life, liberty and the pursuit of happiness.

18

Thomoose did not write this alone.

He had help from many statesmen, and now all that was needed was the stroke of a pen.

19

After 17 days and many drafts,
The Declaration of Independence was completed.

IN CONGRESS, JULY 4, 1776.

The unanimous Declaration of the thirteen united States of America.

Thomoose set sail for France to ask
King Louis XVI to help pay
for the revolution.

While in France,
Thomoose traveled to many countries in Europe.

He brought back ideas about
architecture,
agriculture and science.

When Thomoose returned, George WashingTON had been elected the first president.

George declared, "I think it would be great, if you will be my Secretary of State!"

As Secretary of State,
Thomoose would travel the world
to make friends with other countries.

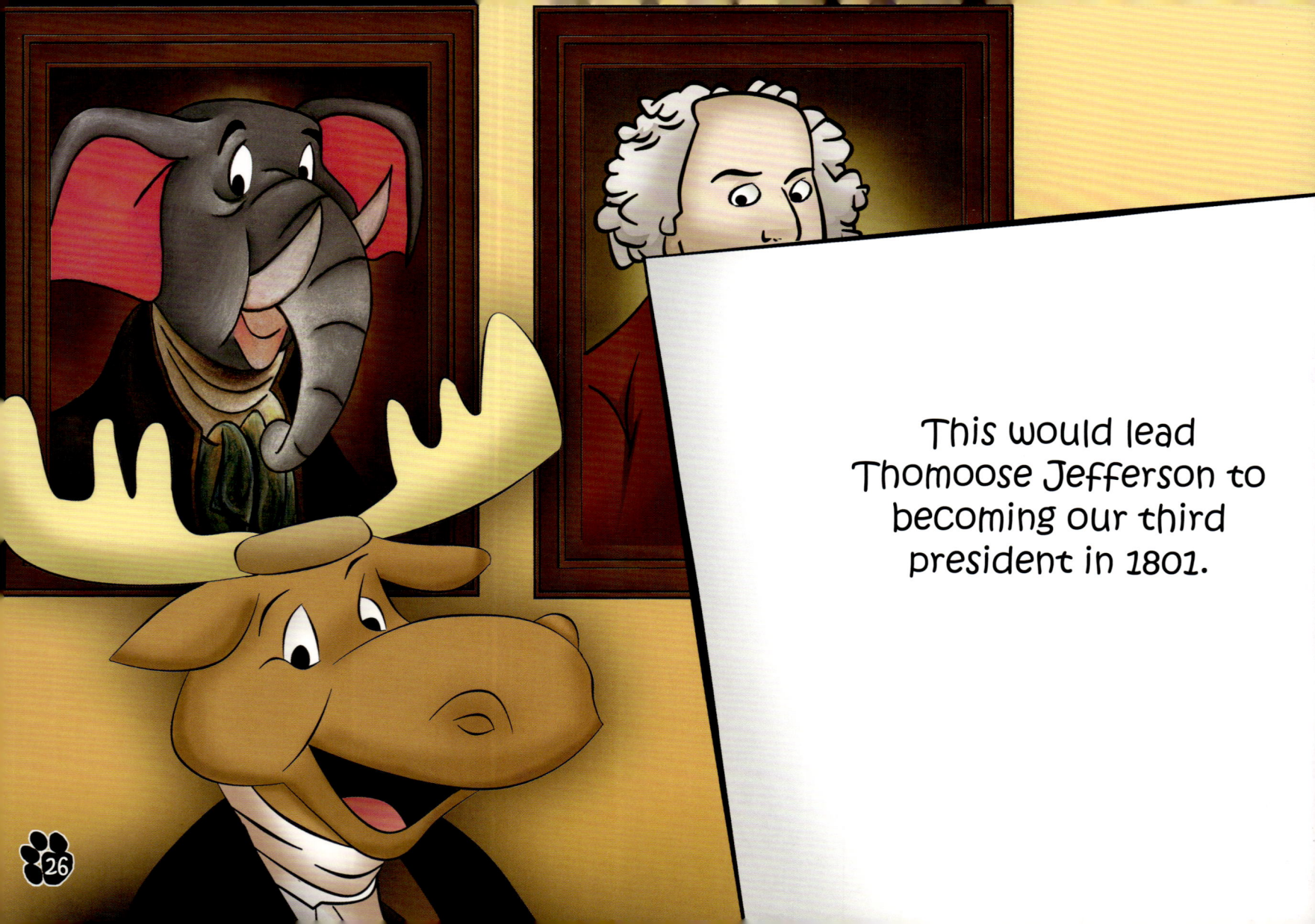

This would lead Thomoose Jefferson to becoming our third president in 1801.

Soon after the inauguration, Thomoose received a message from the French general, Namolean Bonaparte.

It said:
I need more money to fight a war.

Would you like to buy some land to help your country expand?

Louisiana Purchase

After thinking it over, Thomoose made the purchase from France.

The Louisiana Purchase doubled the size of the United States.

28

When his term as president ended, Thomoose returned home to Monticello.

The Library of Congress would be one of Thomoose's great contributions.

It started as a collection of his books and would eventually become the largest library in the world.

The University of Virginia
was Thomoose's next creation
that would live on for generations.

The buildings were of his design
and he hired all the greatest minds.
He wanted this school to be the best
and different from all the rest.

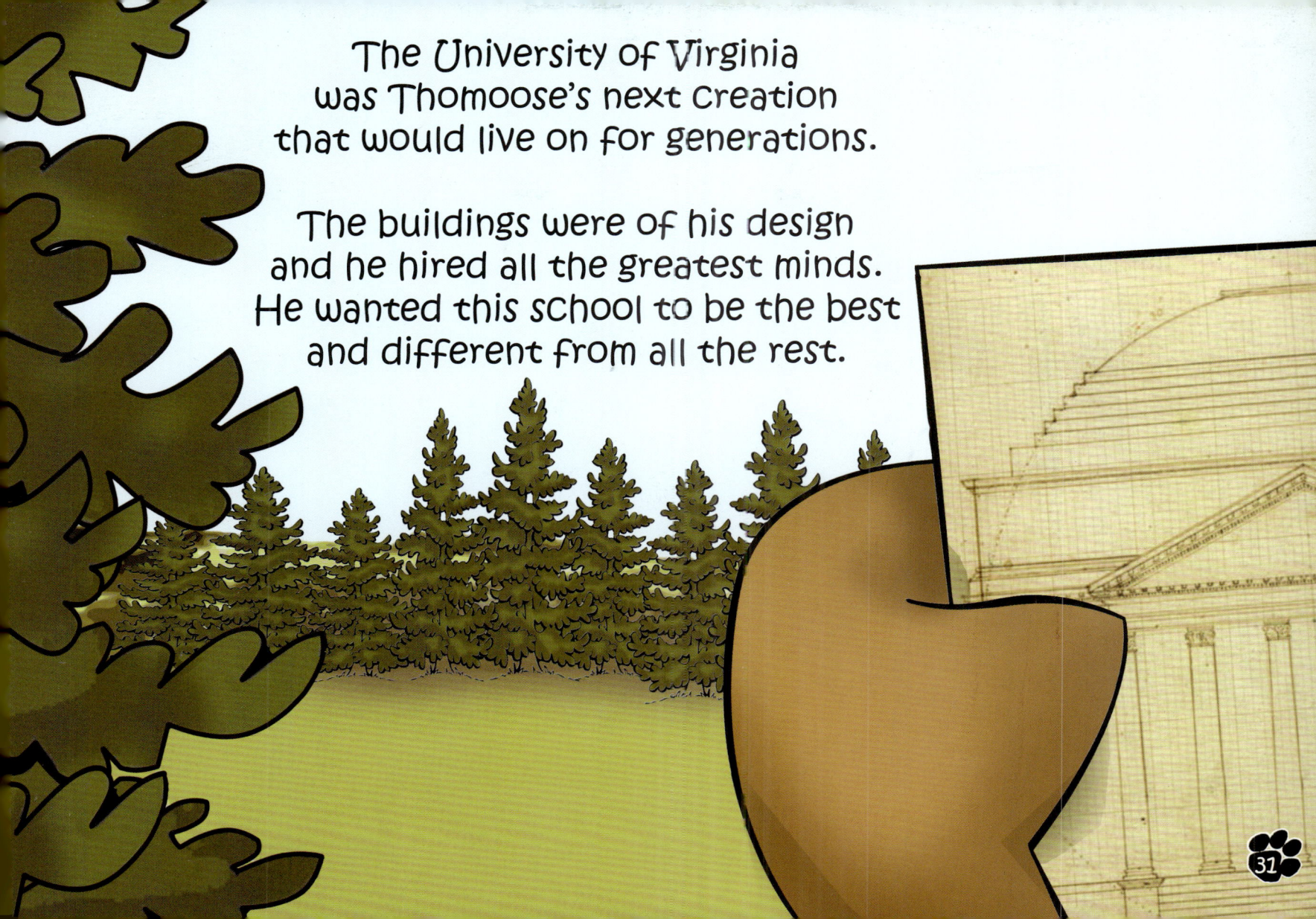

Thomoose Jefferson was the father of liberty.

He had many interests but the most important was his pursuit of truth and justice for all people.

Words to Know:

Agriculture: Noun - the science or activity of farming, includes raising crops and animals for food.

Architecture: Noun - the act or process of designing buildings, or the profession of an architect.

Contribute: Verb - to give for a purpose, endow or lend (money, time, knowledge etc.)

Generation: Noun - the entire group of people who were born around the same time.

Polyglot: Adjective - able to speak or write several languages; multilingual.

Representative: Noun - a person who speaks or acts for a group or community.

Statesmen: Noun - a man who shows skill and wisdom in government.

Studious: Adjective- being devoted to study.

George
Washington
Carfur™

Coming Soon
from
hi·stories ®

Marco Hippolo™

Ludpig Van
Beethoven™

Abrahound
Lincoln™

Juan Ponce De LeBison™

Susan Bee Anthony™

JoHorn Gutenberg™

Bark Twain™   Sir Ibis Newton™   Namolean Bonaparte™